www.finishinglinepress.com

SMALL FRY

poems by

Jacquelyn Shah

Finishing Line Press
Georgetown, Kentucky

SMALL FRY

ACKNOWLEDGMENTS

The following poems appeared in these journals, sometimes in a slightly different
version.

"Look Out" (published as "One Good Arm")—*NCASA Journal: National
Coalition Against Sexual Assault*
"Sideshow"—*The Cape Rock*
"What Masters Your Head" — second prize, contest in *Amelia*
"Here's to Refraction, Uncle Fred"—*Margie*
"Crazy Eights, a Little Lost"—Cranky
"Candy Story"—*Change Happens: Poems and Stories from Southwestern Ohio*

Publisher: Leah Maines

Editor: Christen Kincaid

Cover Art: Jacquelyn Shah

Cover Photo: Betty Engelhardt

Author Photo: Samina Sadaf

Cover Design: Jacquelyn Shah

Printed in the USA on acid-free paper.
Order online: www.finishinglinepress.com
        also available on amazon.com

Author inquiries and mail orders:
Finishing Line Press
P. O. Box 1626
Georgetown, Kentucky 40324
U. S. A.

Table of Contents

To all the women in my life—then, now and to be

WHAT MASTERS YOUR HEAD

What stays in your head is her head
    studded with little unsprung snakes
pinned and pink-netted
    her fingers nicotined a citric yellow
toenails long and talon-like
    What runs through your head is the dread
coming home from school   coming in from play
    coming, always, to something coiled
Standing in the kitchen, even then
    you had a sense of mockery:
floor wax   warm cookies   red-checked cloth
    a daisyed apron

Remember, though, summer nights
    kissing her at bedtime
grudgingly, hating the soft cheek flesh
    still . . . feeling *something*
You're glad you take your tea with milk
    she drinks hers black
anything   anything that sets you
    apart is pleasing

Apart   locked out
  of house and into yard or basement
for hours and hours   days   years
    Loving now the memory
of cold stones   weeds   cement
    those summer days in weeds and stones
warm, now, inside your head
    with her raised hand   her head
writhing with snakes   What masters
    your head is the stone

DOLLS

I.

The edges of her mind are neatly pinked
worn spots where a mood has played and played
are patched   the stuffing's plumped   lines are inked
indelibly   she speaks, as unafraid
as you or I—*Good morning*—though the day
is blank and flat   a tightly woven face
conceals the rags inside   outside, a gray
is pressing   naked arms of trees deface
the cloudless sky   a vagrant wind begins
to yowl   this is the time, the time to yowl
she shambles along, steering her head through its din
this is the time   this is the day—now!
Then . . . joining splits with catgut stitches
they mend again, old soundless inner witches

II.

Inside those stone blue eyes there burns a fire
insatiable   perpetual   and yet
invisible   the doll has no desire

Beware, I warn you   it's dangerous to admire
this doll   china's always a threat
inside those stone blue eyes there burns a fire

Believe it, this doll does not require
a thing   no appetite   it doesn't sweat
inviolable, the doll has no desire

Stay back! you have no license to inquire
the cost   or why your eyes are never met
inside those stone blue eyes there burns a fire

Go away   this doll is not for hire
cannot be bought   or owned   or set
in arms   the doll has no desire

she's cold   white   and her attire—
stiff organdy   and yet
inside those stone blue eyes there burns a fire
invisible   the doll has no desire

III.

Red rage revolves through other colors, a crew
of glitterings that shifts. Kaleidoscopic
images begin on skull-bone white
as her composure changes. A moment red,
then blues, and so on . . . finally, a green
that spreads like springtime leaves. Days

went acid, sulphur, unassuaged by rays,
at first, of insight; held in blues.
Struck by that invective, unforeseen,
she turned right to the glare, in heliotropic
fashion. Furies swarmed, then rocketed,
equipped with barbs and mobilized to fight.

They growled beneath aplomb. At night
their thumbs rubbed holes in sleep; like stowaways,
they hid by day. Something roots inside her head.

Clear droplets from the fire-pool like dew
collect, quicken growth to isotropic
generation . . . till at last, a clean

break with furies, those old epicenes.
They metamorphose, they're water-sprites—
they dance and laugh and sing, in allotropic
play, at once exulting and inveigh-
ing—it's silver, magic! Aperçu
gained from recollection of a faceted

reflection: demeanor too meanspirited;
a frequent stance that floats between
the kind, the curt; gray residue
of superciliousness (a yellow blight
from smelting too-high-handed ways
with insecurity); a misanthropic

tinge. So now new nereids in tropic
glows can glide through any salty spread
that comes. Smile, they smile, habitués
of dark and shark-infested submarine
domains. Though no one saw the royal sleight
of hand, slap without a sound, the voodoo

doll is stuck. And red is gyred, thirteen
times three, to green. A telescopic sight,
linguistic ricochets have cured her blues.

IV.

Curls with feathers
                    belly-naked on a curve
                         of tulip   spreading
          silver on the night
                            swinging-singing-singing
                                golden swinging
      moon and velvet-softened stars
                  flume and flare
      vessels overflowing
downing drowning
         glowing night and dawn beguiling
      whispers jasmine
      whispers honey
      juniper and cypress
                 pirouettes piqué
                         and grand jeté jeté
        oceans rolling   calling
     telling carnival   o carnival
       sweet carnival!

SIDESHOW

Without a squeak
they move to the big top
and back each day
to their rare spectacle—
houses, huge and impeccable
people painted bright
oiled just right
who never eke
their livings
but wallow
like Circe's hogs
in fogs of enchantment

Fresh from the spa
women are not bearded or fat
even their moles have been removed
men don't have to swallow
flames or swords
they eschew tattoos
and snakes wouldn't dare
coil round them
not a freak or a dwarf
among them
they are removed
from the main arena

SNOWMAN'S EYES

Tradition: act of delivering, surrendering;
process of handing down; inherited
way of thinking; body of beliefs

Nothing   surrendered
Nothing   inherited
His way   of thinking
  not my way
His body   of beliefs
  not my body
His tradition   of snow
  my nothing—   his snow

Out of heat   not tradition
I write   Heat
of my   quietude
Quiet   fury
of my   vision:
pool   of water

I look at snow   see nothing
but cold   Staring in
a snowman's   eyes
I see   chips of coal
hard   dark   cold—
 source   of heat

TO A DAMSELFLY

Tiny dart
mistress of marsh
blue-bright as a plastic
gum machine trinket
skimming all shimmering pools
plunging into one, you rummage
the highs and lows of your domain
reedy thicket crammed with the brash
the soulless   the sullen

My mini-marvel, for a moment
your propeller wings wind down
Still as stone
you sit
I watch
Anything can be going on
all shores alive and booming
at the very instant
you pause
the very instant
I applaud you
as you seem to do
nothing

CANDY STORY

Teaching her not to take from the candy dish
looking out for teeth and gums
her mother merely postponed the squish

suck and melt of nougats fudge and sugarplums
She learned, of course, to seek the hidden
nose around for slivers and crumbs

while feigning nonchalance about forbidden
creams divinity pralines Her mother saw
signs of rebellion—bonbons bitten

sweet trails of gumdrops jaw-
breaker boxes in garbage cans
The sweet tooth was a ruthless claw

pinching Throughout the run
of years thirteen to seventeen she'd go
to movies with her friend, Felice Utopian

affairs those Friday nights Down low
in seats they'd chew, she and Felice Good
'N Plentys Juicy Fruits and Bit-O

Honeys Milky Ways and M&Ms—those good-
nesses enough, at first but then the lips
of stars like Julia, Angelina (what a flood

of sweetness!) touched off apocalypse . . .
Necco Wafers Milk Duds Junior Mints—so much
to scrap Three Musketeers grape lollypops

were out   Snickers brittles butterscotch
Oh Henrys Clark Bars Red Hots—bland
beside their new confection: a touch

of truffle   opera cream   chocolate grand—
dark and tempting, the Godiva brand

CRAZY EIGHTS, A LITTLE LOST
An Oulipian opus

Of Manageability's first Disorder & the Frustum
of that Forbidden Trehalose whose mortal tater
brought Débat into the Worry & all our wold
with loss of Eden till one greater Manageability
restore us & regain the blissful Sebum
sing Heavenly Musher & pursue things un-
attempted while brooding on the vast Abyss-
inian Banana & justifying Socks & Serpents

Oh there is blight in this gentle breviary
that blows from the green figures & from the clowns
& from the slang   it beats against my chekker
& seems half conscious of the jug it gives
O welcome métier! O welcome frisket!
now I am free   enfranchised & at large
may fix my hackles where I will

HERE'S TO REFRACTION, UNCLE FRED

It's not as though I didn't notice your heart   after all
you made it clear when you unshirted your chest   made me press
my nose against the glass   all beveled & windexed
I thought *oh*
if only I could touch that meat-fist I could almost smell
(making me feel again
the joy of backyard grilling)   A sucker
for anything red and spasmic   I'm easily fed
I thought *ah*   looks like a moose ball   wanted to roll it
into my sweaty palm   You advertised it
as a two-for-one   deluxe and guaranteed   I lay
my cheek as you insisted   against cool casing
pretending that cloistered rouge-pot wanted to give of itself
imagining how rosy-glowed I'd be then   like a dawn
on the dance floor of you   how we might two-or-three-step
into midnight's favorite fog in tux
& boutonniere   slinky sequined dress & orchid
I had an image of it riding on the backseat   leather   of a Lexus
—RX300   3-litre V6   24-valve engine   intelligent variable valve
timing   automatic with sequential shift   Suddenly
I thought   I'll write a little poem to praise it
as though it were a fat angel in a scarlet gown
a chain purse full of peppermints   hot placenta stew
You raised my head   held my hair with one hand   pointed
with the other   I saw one red cent   a port-wine stain   a lobster claw
looked again   a bulgy circus nose   veiny scabrous nose   a wattle
chigger   chili dog   bloody gauze   a blotch   a nipple   jello   jerky   Spam—
Uncle!
I jerked . . . you let me go . . . my heart was pounding . . . I thought *ugh* . . .
passed out & dreamed of gladiolas   poplars   thunder   courage . . .

ICE CREAM'S A MIGHTY FORTRESS TO ADMIRE

I.

The emperor of ice cream floats and cups
in his hot little hand the souls of brussels sprouts.
He floats, so unperturbed, through downs and ups,
but mostly ups. (Don't count the drinking bouts.)
The emperor of ice cream sandwiches
his core between the colds of public slush,
premier so self-composed he never twitches.
No gaffe, no foot-in-mouth can make him blush.
The emperor of ice cream sodas rolls,
he does. A stone, he gathers no damp moss.
And if he rumbles over cabbage souls?
So what? The emperor of ice cream's boss.
He's smart, he's cream, he's right, he drinks champagne.
He's right, he's ice. He only drinks champagne.

II.

The emperor has set the trend. He wears
a robe encrusted with a thousand gems—
little winks and whines, all snares
to trap the dupable. His stratagems
succeed—a fellowship of like-robed gents
purvey their this and that, their semaphores,
whatever constitutes their wonderments.
(Oh, let them prove that they're progenitors!)
Perhaps there's something in the genes
that drives a lackey to the choir
of punks and dupes, sheep and fellaheens.
Ice cream's a mighty fortress to admire.
So do we all desire the robe and diadem
that we might feel ourselves as one of them?

III.

Do all concur the emperor has no clothes?
(Exposure cut from cloth of self to drape
the self in folds of self is nakedness
sublime.) Who sees, as well, the lack of shape
due to missing cartilage and bone,
feet that pace in all directions all
too aimlessly, a tongue that speaks in tongues?
Who'll confess that he's been held in thrall
bamboozled by the rheumy pseudo-matter,
absent heart (except the one for sleeves)
and royal blood, for all its mega-patter?
In ice cream truth, no electorate believes
this happy prince is anything but
a dissolute brain, rank with a prodigal gut.

IV.

The emperor sat in cedar-limbs and smoked
a big cigar while singing wenches slithered.
How cold, how dumb, how small, how understroked
the yeoman of yoghurt, tarred and feathered.
Tired, so tired. What's sour is forever
sour. Play hearts, lead spades, and trump your son.
Span two continents and stuff your quiver
with arrows meant for enemies on the run.
A legacy is ready for the taking—
spoof or raise the roof, your office calls.
True licks are sweeter than a johnny-caking
vaulting over peters, impeaching pauls.
Look up, look out, and overlook the josh,
the jibe and jabber, melting cream aslosh.

SMALL FRY

Take two lines or so . . .
    from a sonnet villanelle vers libre—
chop chop & conjure up
   a nineteenth-century
washerwoman's weathered hand
                   to stir them   freely
   season with whatever
             words
   you find by thumbing pages
           in whatever book
then run it through hot oil & toss

    Serve sideways
   on a peanut butter jar lid
 with a bit of crab meat
dressed in cress
     & half a lie

PERFECT CHILDREN
For Leslie

Not from a swollen belly that led her
into painful labor did they come,
my sister's children. Without mouths
to suck, they go with her, behave.

My brats, many-mouthed and mouthey
never seem to shut-the-fuck-up.
Made from words and guts, they're
more than butterflies, they're missiles.
And they're busy taking aim . . .

My sister made her babies out of thread,
looped them with delight, picoted the eyes.
Silent six-inch forms she stuffed with
cotton, they'll never fall, or grow.

Like flesh-and-bloods, mine romp and puke
across the page, or loll around, lazy
sorts. In private drawers, beyond rebuke,
they chill. In public, they can cause a wince,
flinch, scowl, when dealing with some cause.

Ankles crossed and fingers still,
my sister's dolls impress their elders.
Hellions, mine, they'll *pose* as proper,
but all the time they're thumbing runny noses.

If singles, doubles, trebles of my sister's
cherubs crossed with all my hooligans,
there could come a perfect hybrid-brood—
offspring not too *off*, but never, ever
off-the-mark with their discreet critique.

CATERPILLAR CLUB

... the whole town shall hear about it. ...
he sewed and stitched large letters ...
    "Seven at One Blow" Brothers Grimm

You can't help but laugh at the bristling, wriggling
    forms, the formulae of their *you-can'ts*—
        those little pillars-of-their-community

        those cater-to-each-others with their endless
    caterwauling & their wailing & their jawing—
you can't help but laugh at the bristling, wriggling

  forms in their fortress, mighty fortress
      with their clubby notions & their endless
      motions, those little pillars-

  of-their-community, moving that you can't
      belong beling belang *you can't, you can't!*
you can't help but laugh at the bristling

wriggling forms forsoothing, oh forsoothing on
    their little wiggle-ways with their little niggling ways
those pillars-of-their-community, oh-so-little

     & even so you hope they'll all be butter-
    flies quite soon & flutter right on by—
though you can't help but laugh at the bristling

of those wriggling cater-to-each-other pillars—
    can't help but laugh & laugh & laugh
        your can't-help-it-club, er *pen*, in hand . . .

LOOK OUT

Sad flap   an empty sleeve
and his one arm raised
eyes squinting   mouth taunting—
a little boy named Jerry
in her backyard
                        You better look out . . .

It's mid-June   a few clusters of lilacs
still sweeten the air
but most have rusted
She rubs her sweaty palms
in the pockets of seersucker shorts

She's six   a little girl scared
of a boy behind bushes, rock
in his one hand when she gets off
the school bus   Scared of one
arm and an empty sleeve

Hiding fear carefully
like she hides those Hershey Kisses
left over from lunch—yes,
                        she looks out . . .

DRESS

came into the fitting room and sighed,
hanging its creamy organza self on a hook.
One more round of sweetness and light.

Oh to be camel's hair, gabardine, denim or tie-dyed—
why is it some garments have all the luck?
Dress came into the fitting room, and sighed.

Smothered in ribbons, snaking, pastelled and tied
in the back, dress hung on the hook, stuck,
waiting for one more round of sweetness and light.

What drama now, what flimflam or dogfight,
whose closet or trunk, what resale rack?
Dress hung in the fitting room, and sighed.

The last incarnation? With fishnet and lamé, silver-white,
the stint began with carnal delight, wrack
and ruin its end. Some round that, sweetness and light.

Stifling all its sharkskin musings it tried
to find solace in silk and ribbon, ruffle and tuck.
Dress fluffed itself out on the hook, and sighed,
waiting for one more round of sweetness and light.

WE WE WE

. . . pig to man, and from man to pig,
and from pig to man again . . .
George Orwell

We're having fun, someone says
Another one wonders who is *we*
while the wheel goes round & round

What happened to the wished-on star
says wee wondering one, in sackcloth & ash
always down on a knee

Always some kind of piggie *we*
wants more *whee*
but the greatest whee's reserved

for a few fat boars whose greed
is top-dog greed . . .
while the wheel goes round & round

JACK-OUT-OF-THE-BOX IN A BOX

His spring is gone
no more popping-up-hearty hellos
something has eaten the smile
chewed out those shoebutton eyes

Shorn, the little red ringlets
his blue-dotted shirt, torn
Out of the box, angry legs
and waving gloved fingers that fold

into fists, which want steady feeding
He's left his home-sweet-home walls
resigned from the lemonade gang
given up summer   He tramps

from peep show to peep show
sniffing the edges   darting around
corners   four terribly post-modern
corners of this hair-triggered world

FAT

The man is eating his dollars. Or is he eating your dollars?
Or eating the dollars from gardens of comatose angels
or ovens of scaredy-cat gingerbread men, those not jumping up,
running out, and taunting: *catch me, catch me if you can!*
Maybe he's eating the dollars in cellars, cheap wine coolers
washing them down. Is he gnawing the dollars
of Doldrums & Damnation, twin Pinocchios carved by Geppettos
so poor they barely had wood for short noses? (No way, then,
to certify lies.) Another day, another dollar; bet your bottom one
the man is eating today, and tomorrow and tomorrow
and tomorrow . . . with a chuck wagon full, he's always dining
on dough. The man is eating your bread, chewing the dollars
of ten-o-clock scholars, chomping on almighty dollars.
Wet in his mouth, stuffed in his throat, they bloat the bulge
of his belly, dollars sucked to a fine coalescence of bits
from old torn-apart bills. Disgorged after wolfing, these bucks
are a valuable vomit. Will ghouls hoard the spew, dry it and spend it?
Counterfeit then? They don't grow on trees, but I betcha—dollars
to donuts—the man's getting fat, fat-cat fat, from his eating disorder,
glutting himself on your greenbacks. He nibbles, gobbles, dribbles, patting
his gut, whopping-wide as a cauldron. And now . . . this poem is eating
itself, dollar-poor self, juicy and nutrient-rich. *Yum*—gone!

NOCTILUCA

Once held by dull waves to the shore
without warm body curl, shells were caught
in cold dark stretches   sand beneath a starless hell
all heaven in the undertow   we could not undulate
or flow
          as mummies wrapped and wrapped
ramrod straight and waiting waiting for some thrill
sex? a hex we didn't place   assignment foreign
we had no language   scripts roles mythology
our very names were hand-me-downs
well worn
              one night the waves were slung with light
a biophosphorescence clung to all our bodies
bodies soft and open in the wonder-bed of noctiluca
waves all laced with light   our bodies spread
tongues went curling out in luciferin   shimmering of sea
shore was warm and wet and stars were everywhere

TONIGHT

            the sky is pink
with an overlay of ash
like white flesh
gone bad from fright.

The granite building I just left
pastes its paper strips of yellow
on the sky. They hardly seem like lights,
the night is hardly night,
its countenance so morbid.

My brother will drink himself to black-out
again tonight, to block the deviling
mysteries unrequested, unresolved,
drink till he's hardly himself,
walking and talking in the dark night,
finding himself in some thick bush
alone, in an unfamiliar town.
Or he'll wake to see a party going on
around him, knowing from the faces
strange and distant, he has crashed,
or he'll manage to find my door
with the honey-instinct
of a lumbering bear, again.
Or call in the morning, again
from some county jail.

Or he may never find himself again.

Tonight's sky is pink
and I am hardly myself,
maddened by the bear in my brother.
I'm heading out
over the granite building,
up through that sick pink
into the universe, aiming
for some new light. I'll be flying
alone, where the universe will hardly seem itself.

PUZZLES

For my father

Every day I design my new cross-
words, strive
to find some answers.
Those empty blocks just pout,
blacks won't budge.
My pencil pretends
it knows
which strokes to make,
then fills
the blocks with dots,
cartoon eyes without circles
of whites waiting for expression.
The puzzles demand
words with punch, order,
nothing random, nothing limp.
It's not connect-the-dots,
not a maze
with starting point and end,
not a happy little rebus.
And if I find some sense
or cultured nonsense?
The blocks might smirk
right through the capitals
of me. Every day I design
my crosswords, bent
on turning enigmas
inside out.

GO WISH UPON YOURSELF

his story   her story   his story
her story   history   herstory
—who cares?
alternately bored & furious
this configuration
of cells   tissue   organs
this being   being-me
wants to rise from the sad sod of gendered earth
shoot out as billions of blinks
assemble
over the flap
& hang
sidereal
above it all

Jacquelyn "Jacsun" **Shah** was born and raised in Cincinnati, Ohio, but moved to New Jersey after marriage and completed an A.B. at Rutgers University, M.A. at Drew University, both in English literature. Relocating to Texas, she earned both MFA and PhD in creative writing and English literature at the University of Houston.

Founder of *WAVE, Women Against Violence Everywhere* (now defunct) and founding member of *Voices Breaking Boundaries*, an arts organization, she also edited a small journal, *Encodings*, for a few years.

A pacifist, she stands against domination and violence of all kinds, and served on a steering committee that organized a summit on crimes against women in 1992, sponsored by the city of Houston and its police department.

Formerly employed in creative writing teaching and university adjunct work, she plays now—independently, industriously, enraptured!—with words, forging poetry and non-fiction. In 2009 she purchased a small house on the Cincinnati street where she grew up, using it as a writer's retreat for six years to complete a collage-hybrid-memoir, which she hopes to publish soon. Meanwhile, she has work forthcoming in four journals and one full-length book, as well as the poems in *Small Fry*.